THE DAILY LIFE OF AN AZTEC FAMILY

HISTORY BOOKS FOR KIDS

Children's History Books

Speedy Publishing LLC

40 E. Main St. #1156

Newark, DE 19711

www.speedypublishing.com

Copyright 2017

In this book, we're going to talk about the daily life of an Aztec family. So, let's get right to it!

WHO WERE THE AZTECS?

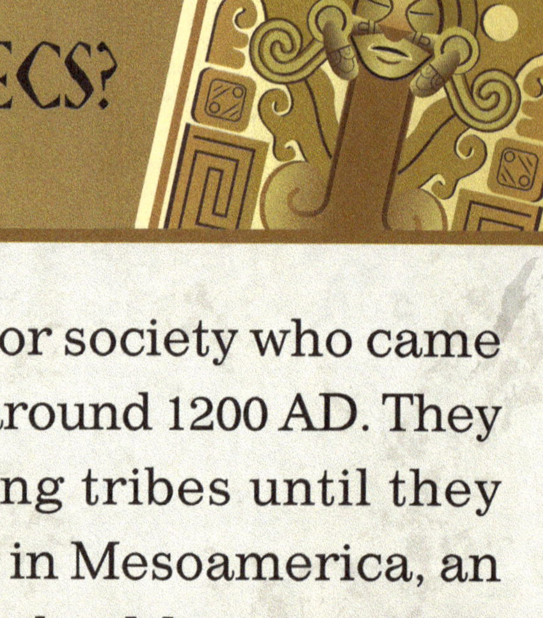

The Aztecs were a warrior society who came to the Valley of Mexico around 1200 AD. They battled with the neighboring tribes until they became the dominant force in Mesoamerica, an area that included modern day Mexico as well as a large portion of Central America.

TENOCHTITLÁN

Just as the Mayan culture had before them, they built enormous cities. The city of Tenochtitlán was built on an island located in Lake Texcoco. Today, this is where Mexico City stands. Tenochtitlán became the central hub of their huge and powerful empire.

Legend says that they built the city on the spot where an eagle was poised on a cactus and killing a snake that it had grabbed up in its beak. The Aztecs built three wide roads to connect the city to the mainland. At the very heart of the city there were three temples.

HUITZILOPOCHTLI

They were all positioned on top of stepped-up pyramid structures. The Great Temple was on one side and then on the top of a second pyramid were two temples, one dedicated to the god of rain who was called Tlaloc and the other dedicated to the god of the sun and war, Huitzilopochtli.

In front of these temples there was a stone platform where the Aztecs offered up human sacrifices to their gods. Once the person was sacrificed, the body was thrown down the pyramid's huge staircase. Many of the people who were sacrificed were prisoners of war from the Aztec's many battles.

The ordinary human Sacrifice.

At the base of the temple structure, there was a round stepped-up temple that was dedicated to the god Quetzalcoatl, the feathered serpent god. Surrounding the temple complex, there were palaces, schools for Aztec warriors, and shrines.

THE AZTEC SOCIAL HIERARCHY

The Aztec culture operated with a defined social structure. This simply means that some people were considered higher class than others. The higher classes had the power and wealth and the lower classes sometimes lived in poverty.

Montesuma

The emperor or king was at the top of the society. The noblemen, who were generally government officials, were next in status as were the priests who performed the temple rituals. The middle class was made up of merchants, craftsmen, and warriors. Those who made their living as farmers or fishermen were not as respected as the merchants. Women were seen as belonging to this class as well. Finally, at the very bottom of the social classes were the slaves.

s in many ancient civilizations, the rich and powerful had pampered lives, but the middle class and lower classes had to work hard every day.

WHAT TYPES OF HOMES DID THE AZTECS LIVE IN?

The Aztec king lived in a palace estate that had a multitude of different rooms, including as many as 100 bathrooms, and a variety of gardens. It even had an aviary and several zoos. Many people were needed to maintain the Aztec king's palace.

The wealthy class lived in homes that had been constructed with stone or bricks that were made of sun-dried mud. They had numerous rooms in their homes with a separate room specifically for bathing, which is similar to today's sauna room. Regular daily baths were a very important ritual in the lives of Aztec people. It was said that the king took four baths every day.

AZTECS

The middle class and lower class lived in small to midsize huts that had roofs constructed from palm leaves.

Some of the houses were elevated off the ground to prevent most types of animals from entering. The houses didn't have doors since theft was very rare.

I n the more modest homes, there was just one big room with sectioned areas. There was an area for cooking, which would have had a flat stone used for grinding up corn, called a metlatl, and a clay dish used for baking tortillas, which was called a comal. There was a small table with figurines of their different gods as a shrine. There was also a section where there were mats for sleeping and an area where they would sit to eat their meals. They had wooden chests to store their clothes.

Comal

Temazcal

Next to most houses there was a temazcal, which was a steam bath. A chimney furnace heated the walls of this room and steam was formed by pouring water over the heated walls. The steam bath provided a place to relax as well as a place to get clean.

Not far from their homes, Aztec families would also have vegetable gardens to grow food and flower gardens for decoration and enjoyment.

WHAT WAS THEIR FAMILY STRUCTURE?

The king had many wives. Usually he would have one main wife who would have the most status. If she had sons, they would be the heirs to the throne. These families got quite large since the wives all had children with the king.

M en of the upper class sometimes had more than one wife, but those of the middle class and lower classes could not afford to have more than one. In these families, the husband generally worked outside the home as a warrior, a merchant, or a farmer. The wife would take care of the children, prepare the food, and weave the cloth for their clothing. Men usually married at the age of 20 and women at the age of 16. Many marriages were arranged by matchmakers.

Depending on their social class, children attended different types of schools. They also helped their mothers and fathers with household chores and gardening.

WHAT DID AZTEC CHILDREN LEARN IN SCHOOL?

The Aztecs had laws that stated that children must attend school. These laws included an education for girls as well as for slaves, which was highly unusual for this time in history. As youngsters, both boys and girls would be taught at home, but when they reached their teenage years they went to a formal school.

AZTEC RUINS

However, boys and girls didn't go to the same schools. Girls were taught the rituals of their religion including ceremonial songs and dances.

They were schooled in how to grind corn and how to prepare food. They were also taught how to weave cloth and sew clothing.

B oys were schooled in farming and fishing techniques or if they were from the families of craftsmen they were taught pottery or decorative work with feathers. If they were to become warriors, they were taught fighting strategies.

AZTECS

Children were expected to have good manners and appropriate behavior. They were not supposed to complain about their schooling or work tasks. They were also expected to have respect for the old and those who were sick. They were taught never to interrupt their elders. If they did not obey, the punishment was strict. Sometimes chili peppers were burned to make a fire that disobedient children were forced to breathe, causing their eyes, noses, and mouths to burn.

WHAT TYPE OF CLOTHING DID THE AZTECS WEAR?

In general, Aztec men wore loincloths and large, long capes. The women wore blouses as well as long skirts. The women were responsible for creating clothing for the family from the cloth they had woven.

AZTECS

AZTEC RUINS

There were detailed rules and laws regarding decorative clothing in Aztec society. Depending on your social class, you were allowed to wear certain types of colors or adorn yourself with specific types of feathers. The king was the only one allowed to wear a cloak that was made from turquoise-colored cloth. Nobles were allowed to wear decorative feathers. The punishment for breaking one of the clothing laws was death.

WHAT DID AZTEC FAMILIES EAT?

Corn or maize was one of the most important foods in the Aztec diet. They ground it and made it into flat tortillas, a process that's still done by natives today. They farmed and ate beans, and different varieties of squash. They ate some foods that we would think are strange today, such as insects, snakes, and dogs. They caught fish to eat and they ate natural honey.

Tortillas

Perhaps their most interesting "food" was chocolate. The Aztecs invented chocolate drinks from cocoa beans, which they brewed using a process that was similar to brewing beer. They thought that their chocolate drink was a food that was worthy of their gods, so it was used in religious ceremonies. In fact the word "chocolate" comes from the Aztec word xocoatl. It was different than today's chocolate in that they didn't use sugar so it was quite bitter in taste.

WHAT TYPES OF GAMES DID AZTECS PLAY?

The Aztecs loved board games and one of their most popular games was Patolli. The players would throw beans to determine their moves around the board. It's a game that requires both luck and strategy.

Patolli

Ōllamaliztli was a popular sport using a rubber ball and played on a court. Players were not allowed to use their hands on the ball. They passed the ball from one team to another using their shoulders, knees, heads, and hips.

ŌLLAMALIZTLI

The Aztec Family are just like any other families in different parts of the world. They have their own way of life and government. There's more to learn about the Aztecs and their interesting way of life.

Awesome! Now you know more about daily life in the Aztec civilization. You can find more History books from Baby Professor by searching the website of your favorite book retailer.

Visit
BABY PROFESSOR
EDUCATION KIDS
www.BabyProfessorBooks.com
to download Free Baby Professor eBooks
and view our catalog of new and exciting
Children's Books